ALIENS!

MARK CHEATHAM

PowerKiDS
press.

New York

Published in 2012 by The Rosen Publishing Group, Inc.
29 East 21st Street, New York, NY 10010

First Edition

Editor: Joanne Randolph
Book Design: Planman Technologies
Illustrations: Planman Technologies

Library of Congress Cataloging-in-Publication Data

Cheatham, Mark.
 Aliens! / by Mark Cheatham. — 1st ed.
    p. cm. — (Jr. graphic monster stories)
 Includes index.
 ISBN 978-1-4488-6222-1 (library binding) — ISBN 978-1-4488-6403-4 (pbk.) — ISBN 978-1-4488-6404-1 (6-pack)
 1. Human-alien encounters—United States—Comic books, strips, etc.—Juvenile literature. 2. Alien abduction—United States—Comic books, strips, etc.—Juvenile literature. 3. Unidentified flying objects—Sightings and encounters—United States—Comic books, strips, etc.—Juvenile literature. 4. Hill, Barney—Comic books, strips, etc.—Juvenile literature. 5. Hill, Betty (Eunice)—Comic books, strips, etc.—Juvenile literature. I. Title.
 BF2050.C465 2012
 001.942—dc23

                          2011027850

Manufactured in the United States of America

CPSIA Compliance Information: Batch #PLW2102PK: For Further Information contact Rosen Publishing, New York, New York at 1-800-237-9932

Contents

Main Characters

Barney Hill (1923–1969) Claimed that he was taken aboard an **alien** spacecraft with his wife, Betty, in 1961, near Lancaster, Vermont.

Betty Hill (1919–2004) Claimed that she was taken aboard an alien spacecraft with her husband, Barney, in 1961, near Lancaster, Vermont.

Dr. Benjamin Simon (c. 1900s) In 1964, Simon used **hypnosis** to help Betty and Barney Hill recover their memories of being taken aboard an alien spacecraft.

About Betty and Barney Hill

- Betty and Barney Hill lived in Portsmouth, New Hampshire. Betty was a social worker. Barney worked for the U.S. Postal Service. They attended a Unitarian Church. Both were members of the National Association for the Advancement of Colored People (NAACP).

- Betty and Barney Hill's story of being taken by aliens was the first story of its kind to gain nationwide **publicity**. Their accounts were well **documented**.

- In 1966, a book was **published** about the experiences of Betty and Barney Hill. It is called *The Interrupted Journey* by John G. Fuller. In 1975, the Betty and Barney Hill story was portrayed in a television movie, *The UFO Incident*.

- In 2008, the University of New Hampshire opened the Betty and Barney Hill Collection. It contains thousands of items relating to their **abduction**.

Aliens!

ERIC AND HIS FRIENDS WERE DRIVING HOME FROM A FOOTBALL GAME ONE NIGHT.

ERIC'S FRIEND SHARON NOTICED SOMETHING IN THE SKY.

WHAT ARE THOSE BRIGHT LIGHTS UP AHEAD?

MAYBE IT'S AN ALIEN SPACESHIP.

I DON'T BELIEVE IN THAT ALIEN STUFF.

OH, YEAH? I THINK BETTY AND BARNEY HILL WOULD DISAGREE WITH YOU. HAVE YOU HEARD THEIR STORY?

"IT WAS THE NIGHT OF SEPTEMBER 19, 1961.

"BARNEY AND BETTY HILL WERE DRIVING HOME FROM A VACATION IN CANADA TO THEIR HOME IN NEW HAMPSHIRE. BETTY SAW A STRANGE LIGHT IN THE SKY."

"THE LIGHT MOVED IN A STRANGE PATTERN THROUGH THE SKY.

"BETTY REALIZED THIS WAS NO PLANE."

NO AIRPLANE MOVES LIKE THAT!

LET'S STOP, AND I'LL CHECK IT OUT.

"BARNEY GOT OUT OF THE CAR TO LOOK AT THE MYSTERIOUS LIGHT.

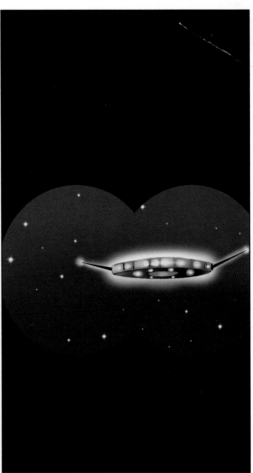

"BARNEY WAS CONCERNED, BUT HE DID NOT WANT TO FURTHER ALARM BETTY."

WHAT IS IT?

I'M NOT SURE. JUST KEEP AN EYE ON IT.

"THEY CONTINUED ON THEIR WAY HOME WITH THE LIGHT STILL FOLLOWING THEM. THE LIGHT SEEMED TO SPEED UP, SLOW DOWN, AND BOUNCE AROUND IN THE SKY.

"SUDDENLY, THE LIGHT APPEARED AHEAD OF THEM ABOVE THE ROAD.

"AFTER COMING TO A STOP, BARNEY GRABBED A GUN HE KEPT IN THE CAR AND JUMPED OUT."

STAY IN THE CAR!

"BARNEY RAN TOWARD THE OBJECT TO GET A CLOSER LOOK.

"WHAT HE SAW WAS CLEARLY NOT FROM THIS PLANET. BARNEY COULD HEAR THE THOUGHTS OF ONE OF THE ALIENS."

STAY WHERE YOU ARE.

"BARNEY JUMPED BACK INTO THE CAR, TERRIFIED. HE KNEW WHAT THE CREATURE WANTED."

THEY ARE GOING TO TAKE US!

"BARNEY TOOK OFF, DRIVING FOR THEIR LIVES.

"BETTY AND BARNEY WOKE UP 2 HOURS LATER AND 35 MILES (56 KM) AWAY.

"THEY HAD NO MEMORY OF THEIR TERRIFYING **ENCOUNTER** ON THE ROAD. THERE WAS NO SIGN OF THE SPACESHIP."

BARNEY, DID SOMETHING HAPPEN TO US?

"WHEN THEY GOT HOME, THEY REALIZED SOMETHING WAS WRONG."

WHAT HAPPENED TO MY **BINOCULARS?**

HOW DID I **SCRAPE** MY ARM? WHAT IS THIS PINK POWDER ON MY HAND?

"FOR SEVERAL DAYS, NEITHER BARNEY NOR BETTY COULD REMEMBER WHAT HAPPENED TO THEM. THEY HAD TERRIBLE **NIGHTMARES.** HOWEVER, THEY COULD NOT REMEMBER THE **DETAILS** OF THEIR DREAMS.

"A FRIEND SUGGESTED THEY SEE DR. BENJAMIN SIMON. HE SPECIALIZED IN HYPNOSIS, WHICH COULD HELP THEM REMEMBER THEIR DREAMS.

"DR. SIMON HYPNOTIZED BARNEY FIRST."

5 - 4 - 3 - 2 - 1

"UNDER HYPNOSIS, BARNEY TOLD THE DOCTOR WHAT HAPPENED TO HIM."

GET AWAY FROM ME!

"BARNEY TOLD THE DOCTOR THAT HE WAS TAKEN ABOARD THE SPACECRAFT WHERE ALIENS DID **EXPERIMENTS** ON HIM."

DO NOT BE AFRAID.

THOSE EYES! WHAT? THEY'RE TALKING INSIDE MY HEAD!

"BARNEY AWOKE IN THE DOCTOR'S OFFICE AND DID NOT WANT TO CONTINUE."

NO MORE, DOCTOR!

"DR. SIMON THEN HYPNOTIZED BETTY TO FIND OUT WHAT SHE COULD REMEMBER."

THEY TOOK US ABOARD THEIR SHIP.

"BETTY SAID THAT THE ALIENS STUDIED BETTY AND BARNEY TO SEE HOW HUMANS WERE DIFFERENT FROM THEM.

"BETTY REMEMBERED AN ALIEN CALLED THE **EXAMINER**. HE DID TESTS ON HER. HE REMOVED SOME OF HER HAIR. HE TOOK SKIN OFF HER ARM.

"BETTY SAID SHE TALKED TO ANOTHER ALIEN SHE CALLED THE LEADER. WHEN HE SPOKE, HIS MOUTH DID NOT MOVE. HE SPOKE TO HER THROUGH HIS THOUGHTS."

WE MEAN YOU NO HARM.

"THE LEADER SHOWED HER A MAP OF WHERE THEY WERE FROM.

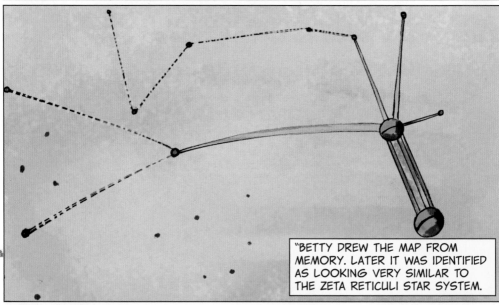

"BETTY DREW THE MAP FROM MEMORY. LATER IT WAS IDENTIFIED AS LOOKING VERY SIMILAR TO THE ZETA RETICULI STAR SYSTEM.

"THE ALIENS BEGAN TO ARGUE AMONG THEMSELVES.

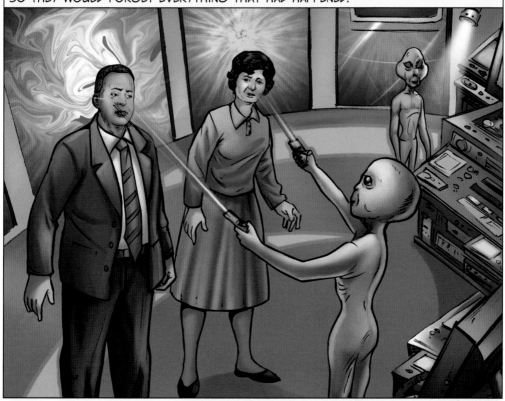

"THE ALIENS DECIDED THE HILLS HAD SEEN TOO MUCH. THEY ERASED THEIR MEMORIES SO THEY WOULD FORGET EVERYTHING THAT HAD HAPPENED.

"THE ALIENS THEN RETURNED THE HILLS TO THEIR CAR.

THE BETTY AND BARNEY HILL STORY IS THE FIRST DOCUMENTED CASE OF AN ALIEN ABDUCTION.

21

More Alien Stories

- **The Crash at Roswell, New Mexico**
  In July 1947, a saucerlike object crashed near Roswell, New Mexico. Mack Brazel, a rancher, happened to be nearby. He saw many pieces of broken metal. Brazel reported the crash to the sheriff. The sheriff reported it to Major Jesse Marcel at the local airfield. The army then released a story to the press saying that a strange saucer had crashed near Roswell. Soon after this, the military released a second statement saying that the "spacecraft" was really a weather balloon.

  At the crash site, Major Marcel collected bits of metal **debris**. He saw strange writing on some of the pieces of metal. The military took the debris away from Marcel. Marcel was later photographed with a weather balloon. Some believe that the picture was taken as part of a story to hide the truth. They think that the military actually recovered parts of an alien spacecraft and the dead bodies of aliens.

- **People Taken by Aliens**
  In March 1973, a waitress named Tammy Stone claimed that aliens had abducted her on her way home from work near Waco, Texas. At first, she had no memory of the event. However, she realized that she had lost 3 hours of her evening. She started having strange dreams about aliens. Over time, she remembered that the aliens had stopped her car and carried her to their ship. There they put her on a table and inspected her. The next thing she knew she was back in her car driving along with no memory of what had happened.

  In February 2008, Terrell Copeland fell asleep on his couch. He woke up in a bright, large room with hundreds of other people. An alien showed him around the room. After his visit to the alien spaceship, Copeland suddenly found himself back at home on his balcony. He saw a large, silver spacecraft speed away. Copeland is convinced that at some point aliens will take special humans, including himself, onto their ships. After the special people are collected, some terrible force will destroy Earth.

Glossary

abduction (ab-DUK-shun) Taking someone away by force.

alien (AY-lee-un) Creature from outer space.

binoculars (bih-NAH-kyuh-lurz) Handheld lenses that make things seem closer.

debris (duh-BREE) The remains of something broken down or destroyed.

details (dih-TAYLZ) Extra facts.

documented (DOK-yoo-ment-ed) To have been written about.

encounter (en-KOWNT-er) A chance meeting.

examiner (ig-ZAM-ner) People who look closely at things.

experiments (ik-SPER-uh-ments) Sets of actions or steps taken to learn more about something.

hypnosis (hip-NOH-sus) A state that people can be put into in which they appear to be asleep but are very open to suggestions or directions.

inspected (in-SPEKT-ed) Checked over closely.

nightmares (NYT-mehrz) Scary dreams.

publicity (puh-BLIH-sih-tee) Public attention or notice.

published (PUH-blishd) Printed so that people can read it.

scrape (SKRAYP) To rub or tear the surface of something.

sessions (SEH-shunz) Meetings.

Index

Web Sites

Due to the changing nature of Internet links, PowerKids Press has developed an online list of Web sites related to the subject of this book. This site is updated regularly. Please use this link to access the list:

www.powerkidslinks.com/mons/aliens/